FOLLOW THE
PROMPTS, SCRATCH
OFF THE PANELS,
RECORD YOUR
THOUGHTS AND
DISCOVER 50 WAYS
TO BE HAPPIER
EVERY DAY

HAPPINESS IS...

CAN YOU DESCRIBE HAPPINESS IN ONE WORD?
SCRATCH YOUR ANSWER INTO THE PANEL

HOW DO YOU FEEL TODAY?

SCRATCH OFF THE BARS
FROM 0–100% TO
REFLECT YOUR MOOD

100%

0%

HAPPY   CALM   HOPEFUL

WHAT CAN YOU DO TO BOOST
THESE FEELINGS?

WRITE DOWN THREE THINGS THAT WOULD IMPROVE YOUR SCORES

1.

2.

3.

WHAT ARE YOU...

MOST
GRATEFUL
FOR?

-

-

-

-

-

-

-

-

-

-

-

-

-

HAPPINESS CAN BE FOUND ALL AROUND US
TRY TO APPRECIATE WHAT YOU HAVE, RATHER THAN
WORRYING ABOUT WHAT YOU DON'T

LIFE IS

DESCRIBE HOW YOU FEEL RIGHT NOW

DESCRIBE HOW YOU WOULD LIKE TO FEEL

SCRATCH OFF ONE PANEL
FROM EACH ROW

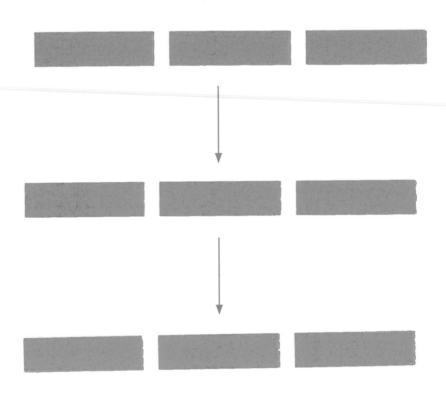

REVEAL A HAPPINESS MANTRA
TO KEEP IN MIND FOR THE
REST OF THE DAY

SCRATCH OFF THE PANEL YOU ARE MOST DRAWN TO

HOW CAN YOU FOLLOW THIS ADVICE?

HOW DOES
HAPPINESS FEEL?

DESCRIBE HOW BEING HAPPY MAKES YOU FEEL

SEARCH FOR MEANINGFUL WORDS
BY SCRATCHING OFF THE BOXES

WRITE DOWN FIVE MORE ACTIONS
THAT ALLOW YOU SPACE TO FEEL HAPPY

SCRATCH OFF
A CHALLENGE

**DO SOMETHING
THAT WILL MAKE
YOU FEEL HAPPY
RIGHT NOW!**

HAPPINESS LOOKS LIKE...

VISUALIZING YOUR OWN HAPPINESS
WILL TAKE YOU ONE STEP CLOSER

DO SOMETHING TODAY THAT YOUR FUTURE SELF WILL THANK YOU FOR

10 WORDS
FOR HAPPINESS

WRITE DOWN TEN MORE WORDS THAT DESCRIBE
WHAT HAPPINESS FEELS LIKE TO YOU

TAKE THE TIME TO FIND YOUR OWN HAPPINESS

WORK ON BEING HAPPY

1 FIND A QUIET SPACE WHERE
YOU WON'T BE DISTURBED

2 SET A TIMER FOR TWO MINUTES

3 CLOSE YOUR EYES AND FOCUS
ONLY ON YOUR BREATHING
UNTIL THE TIMER GOES OFF

SPREAD HAPPINESS

1.

2.

3.

SCRATCH OFF ONE OR MORE OF THE PANELS ABOVE
AND FOLLOW THE PROMPT THAT IS REVEALED

FOLLOW YOUR DREAMS

DO
MORE
OF WHAT
YOU
LOVE

DOUBT

DON'T LET DOUBT STAND IN THE WAY OF YOUR HAPPINESS

"THE BEST
WAY TO
CHEER
YOURSELF
IS TO TRY
TO CHEER
SOMEONE
ELSE UP."

MARK TWAIN

I DESERVE

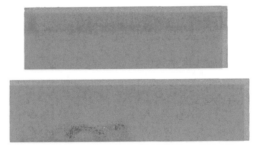

HAPPINESS BOOSTERS

ON A SCALE OF 0–100,
WHICH OF THESE
EXTERNAL FACTORS
MAKES YOU HAPPIEST?

100%

0%

SOCIALIZING

HOBBIES

TRAVEL

WHAT OTHER ACTIVITIES MAKE YOU HAPPY?

WRITE A LIST OF FIVE PEOPLE
THAT MAKE YOU FEEL HAPPY

THEY CAN BE FRIENDS, RELATIVES OR
EVEN PEOPLE THAT YOU HAVE NEVER MET

WHICH OF THEIR HABITS OR TRAITS INSPIRE YOU TO IMPROVE YOUR OWN HAPPINESS

SCRATCH OFF LINES
MAKE LETTERS
SPELL OUT HAPPY WORDS

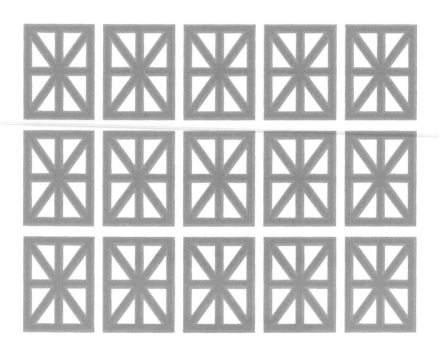

3 STEPS TO HAPPINESS

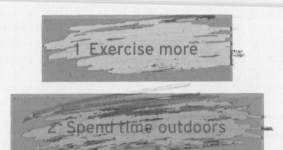

1 Exercise more

2 Spend time outdoors

3 Be kind to yourself

① pole, dance, yoga, bike rides,

② walks, biking, hikes,

③ Positive affirmations, self care, cook for myself,

HAPPY

POSITIVE ACTIONS LEAD TO HAPPINESS

WHAT DO YOU WANT...

TO ACHIEVE
TODAY?

DO

IT

MAKE HAPPINESS A PRIORITY
AND DON'T GIVE UP ON YOUR GOALS

EAT YOUR WAY TO HAPPINESS WITH THESE MOOD-BOOSTING FOODS

1. BRAZIL NUTS
2. BANANAS
3. OILY FISH
4. OATS
5. LENTILS

DID YOU KNOW?

IF YOU ARE NOT FEELING HAPPY, SMILE ANYWAY
IT WILL IMPROVE YOUR MOOD!

ACKNOWLEDGE AND CELEBRATE YOUR OWN ACCOMPLISHMENTS

"HAPPINESS IS WHEN WHAT YOU THINK, WHAT YOU SAY, AND WHAT YOU DO ARE IN HARMONY."

MAHATMA GANDHI

YOU

BELIEVE IN YOURSELF
BE YOUR OWN CHEERLEADER

"THE HAPPINESS OF YOUR LIFE DEPENDS UPON THE QUALITY OF YOUR THOUGHTS."

MARCUS AURELIUS

DID YOU KNOW?

SPREAD JOY BY SMILING AT OTHERS
AS YOU GO ABOUT YOUR DAY

IT IS
BETTER TO
███████████████████████████
THAN TO
███████████████████████████

TRY TO THINK OF WAYS THAT YOU CAN HELP OTHERS

LEARNING A NEW SKILL HAS BEEN
SHOWN TO INCREASE HAPPINESS

WHAT HAVE YOU ALWAYS WANTED TO LEARN?

_____

_____

_____

_____

STAY ███████

WORK █████

BE ████

LIFE IS

COMPARING YOURSELF TO OTHERS
WILL NOT MAKE YOU HAPPY

YOU DESERVE TO BE HAPPY
BELIEVE IT!

WHAT ARE YOUR...

GREATEST
ACHIEVEMENTS?

HOW DO YOU
SEE YOURSELF?

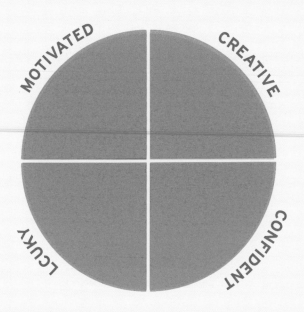

SCRATCH OFF THE SEGMENTS THAT REPRESENT YOU

WHICH OF THESE TRAITS DO YOU THINK CONTRIBUTES MOST TO YOUR HAPPINESS?

"PEOPLE ARE USUALLY AS HAPPY AS THEY MAKE UP THEIR MIND TO BE."

ABRAHAM LINCOLN

HALF FULL OR HALF EMPTY?

SCRATCH OFF THE LEVEL OF THE GLASS
TO REVEAL HOW YOU FEEL

A POSITIVE ATTITUDE WILL
HELP YOU TO FEEL HAPPY

**FIND
YOUR**

WHAT ARE THE FIVE BEST PLACES
THAT YOU HAVE BEEN?

WHAT ARE THE FIVE PLACES THAT YOU WOULD LIKE TO GO TO IN THE FUTURE?

WHERE?

HAPPINESS IS CLOSER THAN YOU MIGHT IMAGINE

"IT'S GOOD TO HAVE AN END TO JOURNEY TOWARD; BUT IT IS THE JOURNEY THAT MATTERS, IN THE END."

ERNEST HEMINGWAY

HAPPINESS IS